# OUTSIDE DOCTOR ON CALL

the *Life-Story* of

EZRA AND FRANCES DEVOL

by

Betty M. Hockett

*To Gary
Betty M. Hockett*

GEORGE FOX PRESS
600 EAST THIRD STREET • NEWBERG, OREGON 97132

To
**DOROTHY AND MARGE**
who encouraged their friend as they traveled
and worked and laughed together
along many miles, through many years.

### OUTSIDE DOCTOR ON CALL

The LIFE-STORY of Ezra and Frances DeVol

© 1992 George Fox Press
Library of Congress Catalog Card Number: 92-071948
ISBN: ISBN 0-943701-20-1

All Scripture verses in this book are from
*The Holy Bible, New International Version,* © 1978
by New York International Bible Society.

*Cover and sketches by Jannelle Loewen*

*Litho in U.S.A. by The Barclay Press, Newberg, Oregon*

# CONTENTS

1. A Sad Christmas .......................... 1
2. Count Me Out ........................... 9
3. Trouble Begins .......................... 17
4. Hope Disappears ........................ 23
5. Difficult Days ............................ 29
6. What Next? ............................. 35
7. The Broken-down Bike .................. 43
8. Two Mad Bears ......................... 53
9. Heading North .......................... 57
10. We've Come a Long Way ................. 67

## The Life-Story from Missions Series

FROM HERE TO THERE AND BACK AGAIN
*the life-story of Dr. Charles DeVol,
missionary to China and Taiwan.*

WHAT WILL TOMORROW BRING?
*the life-story of Ralph and Esther Choate,
missionaries to Burundi, Africa.*

DOWN A WINDING ROAD
*the life-story of Roscoe and Tina Knight,
missionaries to Bolivia, Peru, and Mexico City.*

HAPPINESS UNDER THE INDIAN TREES
*the life-story of Catherine Cattell,
missionary to India and Taiwan.*

CATCHING THEIR TALK IN A BOX
*the life-story of Joy Ridderhof,
founder of Gospel Recordings.*

MUD ON THEIR WHEELS
*the life-story of Vern and Lois Ellis,
missionaries to the Navajo Indians.*

WHISTLING BOMBS AND BUMPY TRAINS
*the life-story of Anna Nixon, missionary to India.*

KEEPING THEM ALL IN STITCHES
*the life-story of Geraldine Custer,
missionary to Burundi, Africa.*

NO TIME OUT
*the life-story of George and Dorothy Thomas, missionaries to
Burundi and Rwanda, Africa, and the Navajo Indians.*

OUTSIDE DOCTOR ON CALL
*the life-story of Ezra and Frances DeVol
missionaries to India and Nepal*

All by Betty Hockett, writer of Christian education
curriculum and stories for children.

# Chapter 1

# A SAD CHRISTMAS

"Please don't put me in the third grade again," begged ten-year-old Ezra DeVol. "I've already been a third grader in three places this year." His face wrinkled into a frown.

Myrta Windsor, a teacher at the Alum Creek, Ohio, Special District Academy, stood before him. Ezra's dark brown hair, carefully parted on the left side, lay smooth against his head. That spring morning he looked as polished as possible. He wore a clean blue shirt and darker pants, neatly ironed. Only a few scuffs showed on the toes of his sturdy black shoes.

Mrs. Windsor shuffled the papers in her hand. She smiled as she asked, "How about fourth grade?"

Ezra's face relaxed. "Oh yes! Thank you, Mrs. Windsor. I promise to work hard."

Ezra kept that promise. Ten days later, the school year ended. He had done well. "We're going to promote you to the fifth grade," the teacher said.

For almost all of his life before that spring of 1920, Ezra had lived in China. In fact, he had been born there. His father, Dr. George DeVol, had died in China soon after Ezra's eighth birthday in 1917. His mother, Dr. Isabella, chose to stay in China to continue her work at the mission hospital the DeVols had built at Luho.

Then, her health turned bad. Dr. Isabella and her children moved to Nanking for the next two years. Her illness progressed. One day she told Ezra and his brother and sister, "We must return to the United States."

After they arrived, the DeVols accepted invitations for long visits with relatives in California, Ohio, and New York. They all thought at first that Dr. Isabella might get well. Instead, she became worse.

The four DeVols then returned to Alum Creek to live with Uncle Elbert and Aunt Martha Benedict at Sunnyslope Farm. Ezra, his sister, Catherine, and his brother, Charles, loved the big white house, the lawn, and the fields. The months went by and Dr. Isabella grew even weaker. By the winter of 1920 she lay dying.

The December days dragged by. Ezra's school friends eagerly compared ideas of what their special stockings might hold on Christmas morning. Ezra said nothing. No one at Sunnyslope had time to hang stockings on the mantel or to plan surprises.

Dr. Isabella grew weaker every day. Grownups tiptoed through the house, whispering about the future of the DeVol children. "A cousin in New York wants Charles to live with him," said one. Another reported hearing from a cousin in Indiana. "She's invited Catherine to live with her."

*What about me?* Ezra wondered. *Doesn't anybody want me?*

On Wednesday night, December 20, the family gathered around Dr. Isabella's bed. She asked in a voice they could hardly hear, "Who will go? Who will help our dear Chinese know the love of God?"

Ezra watched as Catherine stepped forward to say, "I will go, Mother." Charles answered next, "I will go, too."

The youngest DeVol hung back. He could not make such a promise. He had no intention of ending up as a missionary. Donkey-back rides, horrible smells, malaria attacks—he had had enough of all that. He preferred life in the United States. Ezra kept quiet. He did not want to lie to his mother.

Mrs. DeVol died before morning.

"How can I get along without her?" Ezra sobbed. He could not stop crying. Then suddenly, he coughed and sputtered, "What...what...what'll happen to us?"

Aunt Martha pulled him close against her. "You're going to stay right here, Ezra. All three of you. Uncle Elbert and I want you here, and it's what your mother wanted, too."

"I'm glad we can stay at Sunnyslope," he said.

As winter turned into spring, Ezra asked Catherine one day, "How do you stand it without Mother?"

"I pretend Charles and I have gone away from home to boarding school like we did in China," she replied. "Sometimes we wouldn't see Mother for a long time."

Ezra swallowed hard and whispered, "I never went away like that." In the midst of a sob, he blurted out, "Oh, Catherine, I miss her so." Rather than stand there and cry, he rushed off to help Uncle Elbert with the farm chores.

One day Ezra carried a package to school along with his lunch and books. "What's that?" someone asked. "My first-aid kit," Ezra answered. "If anybody gets hurt at recess, I can take care of them. When I grow up I'm going to be a doctor like my mother and father were."

The years passed. Ezra finished grade school. Rather than walk the five miles to high school at nearby Ashley every day, he rode Uncle Elbert's horse named Midget. During those years, Charles married Leora Van Matre and Catherine married Everett Cattell. They moved away to homes of their own.*

After high school, Ezra enrolled in Marion College at Marion, Indiana, where Charles and Leora lived. They invited him to live with them while he went to college. "We'll give you a room and your meals at no charge," they said. Ezra took them up on their offer. In his first year at college, Ezra met another student named Frances Hodgin. At first he

*Read more about Charles and Leora in From Here to There and Back Again, and more about Catherine and Everett in Happiness Under the Indian Trees, both by Betty M. Hockett.

saw her only at a distance, but even so, he thought, *She's really pretty.* He liked the way her light blue hat fit tightly over her short, black hair.

The next time Ezra saw Frances, they had a chance to talk. "I've heard about you," she said. "My father helped at your mother's funeral."

"He did?" replied Ezra.

"Yes. His name is Daniel Hodgin. We lived in Columbus, Ohio, then."

As Frances talked Ezra looked directly into her brown eyes. She stood nearly as tall as he did. He noticed again how nice she looked. Frances spoke with a soft, gentle voice. "But I heard about the DeVols even before your mother died. Myrtle Williams came to our church once and told about their missionary work in China."

Instead of concentrating on what Frances had just said, Ezra thought, *I hope I can get to know her better.*

Frances smiled, and for the first time Ezra heard her laugh. "I loved the stories about how your parents built a hospital there," she said.

*Her laugh sounds like music*, Ezra thought. *I'll have to figure some way to get better acquainted with her.* Quickly, though, he reminded himself, *But, I must study hard so I can get into medical school.*

Ezra DeVol and Frances Hodgin both had to work to earn money to pay their college bills. They managed to find time, though, to take part in school activities. Club meetings and work sessions of the yearbook staff gave them time to talk together.

Sometimes Ezra told Frances about his boyhood days in Luho, China. "I loved watching my father operate," he said. "He taught me the names of all the bones in the human body long before I could read or write."

"I prayed for China when I was a little girl," Frances told him. "I'll never forget the night I said, 'Here am I, send me' at the end of a missionary service at our church."

Ezra liked watching Frances when she talked. He felt uncomfortable, however, when she mentioned missions. Frances also talked about her life as a pastor's daughter. "My father often preached in other churches. He was gone the day I almost died when I was only five. I'll always remember how sick I felt just before I fainted."

Ezra thought her voice had an unusually happy sound to it as she continued. "When I came to, after I fainted, I had the feeling I had been on a long trip to a faraway place — somewhere wonderful and beautiful, full of light and softness. I felt like I had been in heaven. It makes me want to go there."

Ezra sighed. The more he saw of Frances, the more he liked her. Frances liked Ezra better each time, too. She looked forward to their conversations.

Once they sorted pictures for the yearbook. "Here's one of the student prayer meeting," Frances said. Ezra attended Sunday school and church or young people's meetings, but he usually avoided student prayer meetings. He might hear God speak to him there. *I'm not ready for that*, he thought.

One evening in his third year of college, Ezra ended up at the prayer meeting. Just as he feared, God spoke to him. *Lord, If You want me to go forward to pray*, Ezra replied, *show me by asking Bill Emerson to come speak to me.*

A moment later, Ezra's friend, Bill, walked over and put his hand on Ezra's shoulder. "Don't you want to go forward?"

Ezra could hardly believe this lightning-fast answer. He stepped into the aisle and hurried to the altar. Kneeling, he asked God to forgive his sin.

The next morning Ezra stared out his window. The grass looked greener. A new shade of blue decorated the sky. His mind felt clearer and his heart lighter.

"I'm at peace with God," he told Frances later. "I feel like a new person."

"I've been praying for you," she answered.

By this time Ezra and Frances had fallen in love. They announced their engagement a few weeks later.

Ezra attended the missionary convention at Marion College that spring. All at once, he realized during the final service he had become too interested in missions.

*I must get my mind on something else*, he thought. Quickly he crept out of the chapel and fled to his room. Turning on the radio, he flopped onto his bed and flipped through several magazines.

But the music sounded like noise. The pictures blurred on the page. Finally, he could not stand it any longer. *God wants to tell me something,* he admitted. *I'd better listen.*

He dashed back to the chapel. As he tiptoed in, the speaker asked, "Who is willing to give your life completely to the Lord for overseas service?"

It happened as Ezra had thought it would. God said to him, "I want you to go to China as a missionary."

Ezra knew the time had come to say yes. He walked to the front of the chapel and once again knelt to pray. *Yes, Lord, I'll do what You want me to do,* he promised. *But I want to be sure. If within the next three months I get accepted into Case Western Reserve Medical School, I'll know You want me in China.*

Ezra especially wanted to attend that school because his mother had graduated from there. "I hear that about 700 people will apply," he had said to Frances. "The school will accept only 78. I expect it's impossible for me to get in."

The day after the missionary service, Ezra went into Cleveland for an interview at Case Western Reserve. Three weeks later, he received good news.

"I've been accepted," he told Frances. "It's a miracle! But now I don't know where I'll get the money to go to medical school."

# Chapter 2

# COUNT ME OUT

"How much money do you need, Ezra?" asked John Johnson, a cousin to Dr. Isabella DeVol.

"Six-hundred dollars a year," Ezra replied. "I can stay with Catherine and Everett. That'll help keep my expenses down."

John answered quickly, "I'll loan you enough money for two years."

Another miracle. Ezra told Frances about it that evening. "I asked God who I should talk to about money for medical school, and I thought of my mother's cousin. I had no idea he would answer so quickly."

On June 6, 1932, Ezra and Frances graduated from Marion College. He went on to medical school in the fall. She lived with her parents in Michigan and hunted for a teaching job.

It turned out that Frances could not find a job as a teacher. Instead, she did housework for a family who paid her three dollars per week, plus giving her a room and meals. She helped her father with music when he preached at special meetings. Frances often wrote a letter to Ezra or got one from him.

Ezra had to scramble to keep up at medical school. When he felt discouraged, he took time to look at his mother's picture, which hung in the university hall. Seeing her picture there beside others from the class of 1897 gave him courage.

One day near the beginning of Ezra's second year at Case Western Reserve, Dr. Wiggers called him into his office. "DeVol, you don't have what it takes to be a doctor. Unless you hire a tutor, you have no chance of finishing with your class."

Ezra stood glued to the floor. He did not know what to say. Finally he forced his legs to take him out of Dr. Wiggers's office. He plodded through the day, feeling as if he carried a heavy weight strapped to his shoulders.

Hire a tutor? Impossible. Tutors charged ten dollars an hour. Not finish medical school? A terrible thought. God had answered so many prayers and done so many miracles. Why had it turned out this way?

For ten days Ezra's mind turned these thoughts over and over. Days looked as dark as the nights. Then God said to Ezra, "Do you serve Me because I'm getting you through medical school or because you love Me?"

"Because I love You," Ezra replied.

"Then go back home and be a failure for My sake."

*I can't do that*, Ezra thought. *But if I have to quit medical school, I'll go to California or some other place where people don't know me.*

God knew Ezra's thoughts. "No," God said. "I want you to go back to Alum Creek. I want you to go to church and Sunday school and young people's meetings. Show them you're willing to be a fool for Me and keep sweet about it."

*The hardest order I've ever had*, Ezra said to himself. "All right, Lord, I'll go back home and be a fool for You." For the first time in ten days, Ezra felt relieved.

On his way to class the next morning, Ezra stopped at the bulletin

"When I grow up I'm going to be a doctor like my mother and father were," said Ezra.

board to look for new announcements. Dr. Wiggers stepped up beside him. He put his hand on Ezra's shoulder and said, "It's all right, DeVol. Forget what I told you the other day. You're doing okay."

*God was only testing me,* Ezra thought. *He just wanted to make sure I was willing to do what He asked me to do.* That day a lasting friendship began between Ezra and Dr. Wiggers.

Every week the pathology professor gave a difficult exam to his class. The students sat four at a table. "We'll help each other during the exams," suggested one young man at the same table as Ezra.

"I can't cheat like that," said Ezra. "Count me out!"

Ezra failed the next three exams. Back at the Cattell's parsonage home at night, he prayed. He also wrote to Frances. *I'm about to fail the course. If I do, I'll have to quit medical school.*

He prayed again and again. One day he stopped suddenly. *Ezra,* he told himself, *you can't expect God to work a miracle and give you a passing grade only because you prayed. You've got to study harder. Then you'll know the subject better.*

Once, as he read his Bible, the words of Isaiah 50:7 caught his attention. "Because the Sovereign Lord helps me, I will not be disgraced. Therefore have I set my face like flint, and I know I will not be put to shame."

"That's exactly the verse I needed," he said cheerfully. "Now I can really get to work."

Ezra passed the rest of the exams and finished the pathology class with a good grade.

He missed Frances a lot. *Have you ever thought of studying to be a nurse?* he asked in one letter. *You could come to the Frances Payne Bolton School of Nursing right here at Case Western Reserve.*

This new idea startled Frances. She thought about it awhile, then said, "I'm willing to be a nurse if that's what God wants, and if Ezra does, too."

The next time she talked to Ezra, she told him what she had decided. "But I don't have any money," she added.

"Go ahead, anyway," he suggested, "and take the tests to find out if you can get into the School of Nursing."

Frances did, and she passed. The school accepted her.

A few days later she went to visit Ezra's sister, Catherine Cattell. Two nurses happened to be there, also.

"I've just been accepted into the School of Nursing," Frances explained. "But I won't be able to go because I don't have any money."

"I didn't have any money either," one of the nurses confided. "I got a scholarship, though."

"It's too late for a scholarship now," said Frances. "The term has already begun."

The next day Everett Cattell took Frances to apply for a job at Cleveland Bible Institute. On the way, they passed Case Western Reserve University. Everett suggested, "Frances, why don't you go in there and see if there's a chance for a scholarship?"

Frances shyly entered the dean's office. She told him her situation. Before she left, the dean said, "We'll give you a scholarship for all three years of the nursing course."

Four days later, she began classes. "With God's help, I believe I can be a good nurse," Frances told Ezra.

The Sunday schools of Ohio Yearly Meeting of Friends promised to send money to pay the medical school expenses for Ezra's junior and senior years. Other people also sent two or four or five dollars now and then. Occasionally he received as much as fifteen dollars at a time. Sometimes Ezra sold a pint of his blood for transfusions, earning a small amount of money.

As the end of his senior year drew near, Ezra needed four-hundred dollars for examination and graduation fees. "I don't have any idea where it will come from," he said, frowning.

"God has met all your needs before," Frances reminded him. "Let's pray about it."

Right after that, some of his friends gave money to Ezra. Even people he did not know sent money, also. At graduation time that spring of 1935, he said, "I've received four-hundred three dollars and ten cents."

Dr. William Ezra DeVol began his internship at the Cleveland City Hospital. Frances continued with her nurse's training. At last they could plan their wedding.

It took place in Brighton, Michigan, on August 15, 1936. The congregation included Everett and Catherine Cattell, soon to leave for missionary

service in India. Charles and Leora DeVol sent greetings from their mission station in China.

Ezra and Frances did not have time for a honeymoon. She went back to school right after the wedding, and he had to work at the hospital.

That fall, Frances graduated from the School of Nursing. "We've reached our goal," they told each other. "Now we can get ready to go to China."

They applied to the Ohio Friends Board of Missions, which accepted them. Soon after, they made an important announcement. "We're going to have a baby."

They changed the announcement later. "Our doctor says we're going to have TWO babies."

By that time, Ezra had worked for several months at the Fairview Park Hospital in Cleveland, Ohio. His employer said one day, "I want to promote you to the position of Chief Resident."

Ezra and Frances prayed about it. Then Ezra said, "Being Chief Resident might keep us from going to China." A few days later, he resigned his job. They moved to Michigan to live with Frances's parents until the birth of their twins.

Soon, news arrived that turned their plans topsy-turvy.

## Chapter 3

# TROUBLE BEGINS

"The Japanese and Chinese have gone to war with each other," said Ezra. "We can't go to China now."

He and Frances stared at one another. No job. No home of their own. Two babies coming. What now?

After the birth of their twins, Patricia Lee and Priscilla Ann, Ezra and Frances moved in with Uncle Elbert at Sunnyslope. Aunt Martha had gone on to heaven sometime before.

Dr. G. T. Matthews of Columbus, Ohio, said to Ezra a few weeks later, "I need an assistant. Will you consider working with me?"

*This is the answer,* Ezra thought. Frances agreed.

Ezra's patients soon discovered he would care for them in their homes, as well as at Dr. Matthews's office. They did not hesitate to call on him, even at night. He not only treated their ailments, but he also listened to them and prayed with them.

Ezra operated on eleven-year-old Esther Garner one day, taking out her tonsils. Afterward, Ezra carried Esther to his car, drove her home, and carried her upstairs to her bed.

This extra attention impressed Mrs. Garner. Sometime later she said, "Dr. DeVol, my daughter Martha needs her tonsils out. Will you do the operation?"

As time went on Ezra did not always agree with some of Dr. Matthews's methods. In 1939, Ezra said to Frances, "I think it's time we open an office of our own. I've had enough experience now to do that."

He and Frances rented rooms and soon had a doctor's office ready. "I'll need a car if I'm going to call on patients in their homes," Ezra said. The next week he bought a used car for sixty-five dollars.

Immediately Ezra had a full schedule of patients. He took advantage of every opportunity to tell them that God loved them. "This is the most important part of my work," he said. Sometimes Frances said, "I wish I could be your office nurse."

"There'll be time for that later," Ezra replied. "Right now the girls keep you busy enough at home. Your prayers and your love help me a lot, you know."

Life went on in this way until the next spring when they received good news from the Mission Board. "Conditions in China have improved. We want you to go to China to work at Peace Hospital in Luho."

They sold the medical practice to another doctor, collected most of the money patients still owed Ezra, and packed their belongings. A few days after the twins celebrated their third birthday, the four DeVols said goodbye to their family and friends in Ohio.

They traveled first to San Francisco, California. There, they boarded a Japanese ship, the S.S. *Asama Maru*. When they got to Japan, they changed to another ship, the S.S. *Nippon Maru*.

The big ship edged into the Shanghai harbor several weeks later. Ezra told Frances, "I can't wait to show you around. I'm sure I'll still recognize all the places."

Frances laughed. "This will be fun to have my personal guide."

As the passengers prepared to leave the ship, strong winds quickly developed into a typhoon. "We can't go ashore now," said Ezra as he grabbed Pat. "Frances, you hang on to Pris."

Back in their stateroom, they huddled together in the bottom bunk. Outside, the winds whipped up heavy waves that pounded against the S.S. *Nippon Maru*. The ship tipped one way, then the other. The twins cried as the storm grew noisier and more violent. Ezra and Frances prayed.

"What a welcome to China!" exclaimed Ezra. "I wonder if the storm's going to wash us ashore?"

The storm gradually blew itself out a few hours later, and the ship rested quietly. The DeVols gathered on deck with other passengers in time to hear the announcement, "You may now go ashore."

Patricia and Priscilla clung tightly to their parents' hands as they all walked down the gangplank. Charles and Leora DeVol and another missionary, Charles Matti, ran to meet them.

The two DeVol brothers hugged each other. "I thought we might have to swim to get here, after all," laughed Ezra.

Charles shook his head. "That was quite a storm." Moments later, he said, "I hate to tell you this, but there's still a lot of fighting here. It really isn't safe, yet."

Charles Matti added, "In fact, the American Embassy has urged all Americans to return to the United States."

"But we've only just gotten here," said Frances with a sigh.

"How can we even think of leaving?" Ezra wondered aloud.

"It's hard to tell what may happen," said Charles DeVol.

None of them wanted to leave. In the end, they decided to go to Nanking on the train as planned. They sloshed along flooded streets to the railroad station. Japanese soldiers lined up on both sides of the bridge leading to the train tracks. As people passed them, the soldiers sprayed everyone's legs and shoes with disinfectant.

Frances and the girls hopped as the cold spray hit their legs. "Why did the soldiers spray us?" Frances whispered to Ezra.

"I don't know," he replied.

In Nanking, other missionary friends welcomed the DeVols. A few days later they went on to Luho. There, the newcomers had a lively welcome from Margaret and Esther, the young daughters of Charles and Leora.

"Ezra, our church people have planned a dinner here at noon today in honor of your return to Luho," said Charles.

Soon, many small tables with four or six people sitting at each nearly filled the DeVol house. The servers began to bring out small dishes of food, one at a time. The duck, chicken, pork, beef, fruit, vegetables, fish, and eggs, all cut into small pieces for eating with chopsticks, seemed endless.

The host at each table graciously picked out the nicest chunks of food and placed them on the guests' plates. The servers quickly replaced every empty dish with a full one.

During the meal, someone handed Ezra the tail of the rooster. "That's because I'm the guest of honor," he explained to Frances.

By the middle of the afternoon, Ezra and Frances had sampled thirty-two dishes. "They've done this more in honor of my father than for me," said a stuffed Ezra. "The Chinese loved him."

Ezra took Frances on a tour of Peace Hospital the next day. "Did I ever tell you, Frances, that the

Chinese call a surgeon the *outside doctor*? They call a doctor of internal medicine the *inside doctor*."

Frances listened as Ezra continued. "Let's say a man gets shot with an arrow. The *outside doctor* cuts the arrow off at the surface of the skin. The *inside doctor* gets the rest of the arrow out."

Soon, Ezra and Frances returned to Nanking to begin language study. "We hope we can stay in China in spite of the fighting," they said.

An announcement from the American Embassy quickly erased their hopes. "All women, children, and men who are not engaged in essential work must leave. The S.S. *Washington* will be here to transport you out."

"Since I don't have a permanent hospital assignment here yet, I'm classed as not essential," said Ezra.

The experienced missionaries advised him, "You'd better go back to the U.S. with Frances and the girls."

Ezra replied softly, "Yes, I suppose that's best."

He and Frances began to put their clothes back into the trunks.

They prayed together. They prayed separately. Ezra read certain Bible verses. Afterward, a troublesome idea grew into something he did not want to think about.

He knew, though, he would have to discuss it with Frances.

## Chapter 4

# HOPE DISAPPEARS

"I believe God wants me to stay in China," Ezra admitted to Frances. "But I can't bear the thought of being here without you."

"God already told me the girls and I are to go back alone," Frances replied quietly. "I didn't think I could, but God promised it will be all right."

Sometime later, they all boarded the launch taking the passengers out to the S.S. *Washington*. As the little boat pulled alongside the big ship, Ezra and Frances found it nearly unbearable to say goodbye.

When would they see each other again? They had no idea.

"Daddy! Daddy!" cried Patricia and Priscilla. "Why can't you come with us? We want you to." They watched and waved from the ship as long as they could see any bit of Ezra waving from the launch.

Frances waved, too, remembering God's promises. "I couldn't go on this long journey without your daddy if I didn't know that God will be with us," she whispered to the twins.

Loved ones welcomed them when they arrived in Michigan a few weeks later. No hour passed but what Frances thought of Ezra and prayed for him.

After visiting Frances's parents at Brighton, Michigan, the three DeVols moved to Tecumseh. They lived with special friends, Ella and Edward Escolme. "There are better jobs here," Frances said.

Before long she went to work as a nurse in a Tecumseh hospital.

Meanwhile in China, Ezra remembered how he had suffered as he watched the S.S. *Washington* sail away with his family.

That day as he stepped back onto land, he had thought he might die of loneliness. He trudged to the train station and soon boarded the train for Nanking. Ezra found a group of empty seats and slumped into one of them. *I'm totally alone*, he thought. That day so far had been the worst one of his entire life.

All at once it seemed as if Jesus sat down in the empty seat beside him. "I'm going to Nanking with you," Jesus said.

Ezra's eyes filled with tears as he thought, *The Lord really cares for me. He came to me personally when I was feeling so forsaken*. He managed to smile as he said, "Thank You, God, for being with me."

Settling into Nanking, Ezra thought about Frances and the girls dozens of times every day. He

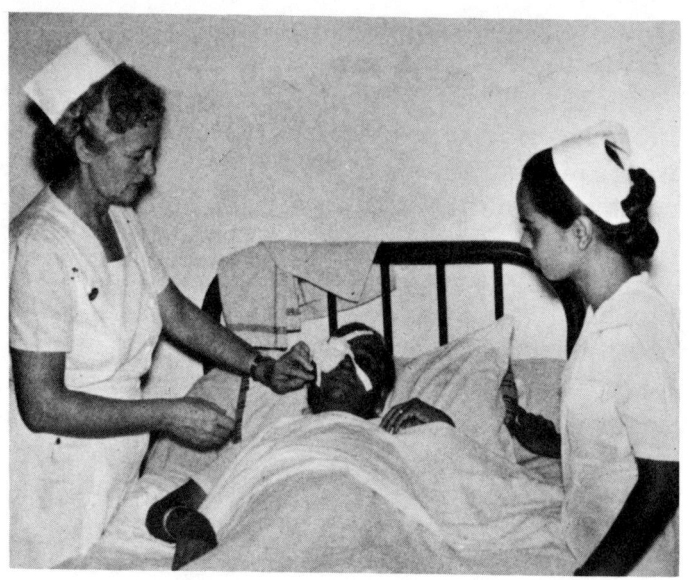
*Frances DeVol and a student nurse attending to a patient*

and other missionaries lived at the mission house called the Quakerage. Now that he had no hope of going to work in the hospital at Luho, he began duty at the University Hospital near the Quakerage. The war had forced some hospitals to close. This one, however, with 180 beds, plenty of medicine, equipment, and nurses had stayed open. The Japanese had taken charge of every department.

One day a young woman came to the hospital with her face so swollen she could not open her mouth. Ezra examined her and said, "You have tuberculosis of the tonsils." He removed them, and she quickly improved.

"Thank you very much," she said to Dr. DeVol. Then she showed him a Bible. "This is what I'm reading."

Every time Ezra visited her after that, he saw her reading the Bible. "I don't have time to read anything else," she said. Before she left the hospital, she became a Christian.

One man arrived at the hospital with a broken hip. Ezra helped make a special splint. It had a device to hold the man's leg up at the proper angle for healing. This man spent a long time in the hospital. While there, he heard about Jesus, who could forgive his sin.

After he became a Christian, the man said to Ezra, "Please take a picture of me here in this bed. It's because of this injury that I heard about Jesus."

Sometimes Ezra thought longingly of Peace Hospital in Luho. "But at least I can still be a missionary here," he said.

One day Ezra discovered an old, broken X-ray machine in a room no one used. "What's that thing doing here?" he asked.

"We put it in there to get it out of the way," a nurse explained.

Soon, a Japanese worker also discovered the unused machine. He thought it looked suspicious. Several Japanese soldiers arrived the next day to look it over. Representatives from the navy appeared and wanted to see it, too. Military police and Japanese civilians showed up later to take their turns at examining this suspicious item.

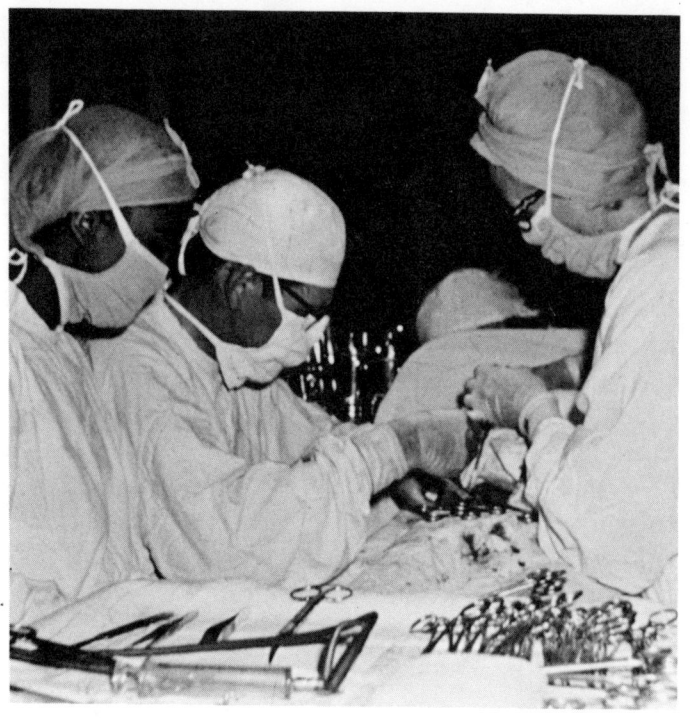

*Dr. Ezra DeVol; Frances DeVol, nurse; and a helper at work in the United Mission Hospital in Kathmandu, Nepal*

"They think we use it to send secret messages," Ezra told the other missionaries. They all had a good laugh about this serious investigation.

Ezra constantly wondered about his family. How much taller had Priscilla and Patricia grown? What did Frances do every day to keep busy? He knew she worried about him. *She also prays a lot for me*, he thought confidently, and prayed for her again.

As the months went by the missionaries finally decided they should return to the United States.

Ezra made plans to leave. He soon discovered, however, his exit visa had expired. He tried to get it renewed, but no one would give him this important permission paper. He could not leave Nanking without it.

Charles arrived from Luho alone, since Leora and the girls had already gone. "I'm going to Shanghai to get a reservation on the ship," he said to Ezra. "I'll get one for you, too."

"I'll be with you as soon as I can get my exit visa," Ezra replied.

Then, on December 7, 1941, he received permission to leave Nanking the next day. Ezra thanked God and packed his suitcases.

But Charles Matti came to him the next morning and reported, "The Japanese have bombed Pearl Harbor. We can't leave now after all."

## Chapter 5

# DIFFICULT DAYS

"Where's Ezra?" sobbed Frances when she heard the news about Pearl Harbor. "Oh, what's going to happen now?" She covered her face with her hands and cried even louder, "I can't stand it!"

Ella Escolme gently gathered Frances into her arms. She spoke softly but firmly. "Yes, you can, Frances."

Ella's strength helped Frances relax little by little. Yes, she would trust God to get her through these difficult days.

\* \* \*

Gloom settled over Ezra in Nanking, now that World War II had started. But God promised him, "I'll go with you through this change of plans."

Ezra straightened his shoulders and thought about what to do next. After a while he hired a rickshaw to take him to the American Embassy. Japanese guards stood all around with rifles aimed at Ezra's belt buckle.

"May I go into the embassy?" he asked.

"No!" barked a guard.

Ezra whirled and ran to the rickshaw. "Please take me back to the Quakerage," he said.

There, the missionaries asked each other, "Will the Japanese soldiers take us to a concentration camp?"

"They probably will," one of them said. "We'd better get ready."

"What shall we take with us?" Ezra asked.

"Lots of food," someone suggested. They began to load food into suitcases.

"It's bound to be cold wherever they take us," one of the men said. They tossed out some of the food and tucked in more long underwear and woolen sox.

As nighttime approached, they remembered to turn out all lights. The Japanese had announced that soldiers would shoot anyone who allowed even a glimmer of light to show. The missionaries banded together in one room, talking and praying.

The soldiers waited until the next afternoon to show up at the Quakerage. Mrs. Matti greeted them graciously. She invited them to sit down in the living room while she served tea.

"We're sorry to announce that our countries are at war with each other," said one of the Japanese soldiers. "We must ask you to sign a statement that you will not spy on us or send messages. We give you permission, though, to stay here in your own home."

*Frances DeVol visiting with her royal highness Queen Ratna of Nepal*

The missionaries followed the orders and settled down to wait for the war to end. Eight days later a Japanese soldier drove up and parked the hospital ambulance in front of the Quakerage.

"Dr. DeVol, you are to come back to work at the hospital," the soldier announced.

"I don't know if I want to work for them or not," Ezra told the missionaries. "It doesn't look like I have a choice, though."

Ezra moved in with another missionary, Dr. C. S. Trimmer of the Methodist mission. "We're the only two Americans here at the hospital," he said.

They had no money to buy anything, and the weather turned bitterly cold. To keep warm, they put on all the clothes they had. One morning Ezra laughed at the way he and Dr. Trimmer looked.

"We're both as fat as Santa Claus with all these things on," he said.

The doctors cared for patients in the hospital as best they could while the Japanese watched closely. Ezra never knew what the new supervisors would say.

One day they insisted, "Erase all the English names for the medicines and label them in Chinese."

"But there aren't Chinese names for some medicines," groaned Ezra. "Morphine, aspirin, or castor oil, for instance."

Men from the Japanese navy, army, and military intelligence came every little while to inspect one thing or another. Even ordinary Japanese people made endless inspections. Every day Ezra wondered, "What'll they want to see now?"

The Japanese superintendent of the hospital treated the doctors kindly. "Let me know if you need medical supplies," he said. "I can get them from Shanghai."

Later Ezra said to Dr. Trimmer, "Sometimes I wonder if the superintendent is a Christian."

Thoughts of Frances and the twins filled Ezra's mind every hour of every day. He wished he could write letters to them. "I'd like to get a letter from them, too," he mentioned to Dr. Trimmer one evening. "But the Japanese have said 'no letters.'"

The Japanese did, however, allow the hospital prayer meetings to continue. Ezra noticed the

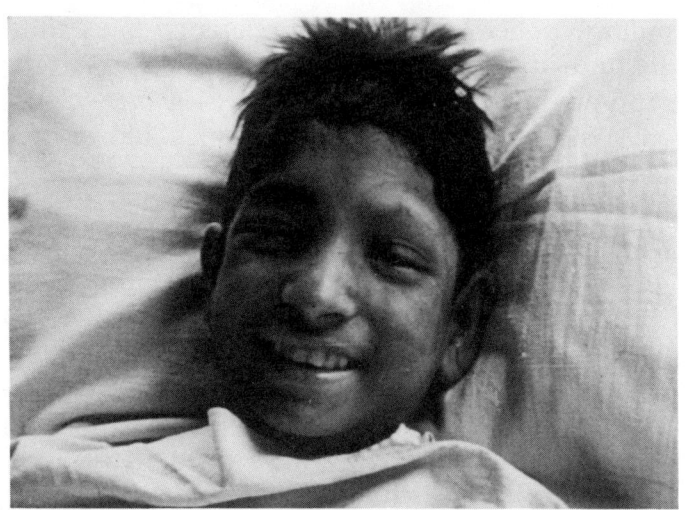

*Chullu after the successful operation*

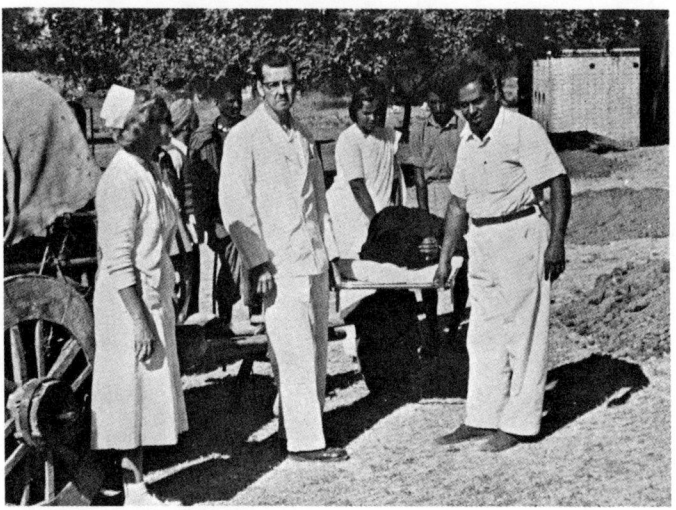

*Ezra and Frances DeVol helping to receive a patient from the village*

military police making an appearance every time, also. *They want to see who comes to pray*, he thought.

Chinese Christians did all they could to help the two Americans have what they needed. They brought food and stayed to pray with them. "Our Christian people are still trying to obey God," they reported to the missionaries. "It's hard, though."

Mr. Hsia (SHAW), a wealthy banker, handed twelve dozen eggs to Ezra every other week as he brought his daughter to the hospital for special treatments. He sometimes included cakes and other tasty items. Ezra always divided the food with the other missionaries and workers.

One Chinese woman said, "I'll gladly sell my donkey and give the money to you."

Tears came into Ezra's eyes. "Oh, no," he said. "But thank you, anyway. You keep the donkey. You need him yourself."

Their Chinese friends kept coming, even after the two Americans advised, "Don't come. You'll only get into trouble."

Then, a rumor started: Some Americans could leave soon.

New hope washed over Ezra, but it quickly disappeared. A Japanese official pointed at him and said, "Maybe some of the old, white-haired missionaries will go, but not you. You are of military age. You'll stay here for the entire war."

## Chapter 6

# WHAT NEXT?

"I'll get ready to leave, anyway," Ezra told Dr. Trimmer, "just in case. But I'm particular about who gets my expensive surgical instruments and medical books."

A friendly Chinese man agreed to smuggle them out and sell them. "I'll put several instruments or books in the bottom of my big, long basket," he told Ezra. "Then I'll sprinkle broken glass over them and lay fresh fruit on top. Each time I pass a barrier, I'll give some bananas or oranges or apples to the Japanese guards."

He came back later to report, "No one ever tried to dig down to the bottom of the basket." The man sold many of Ezra's things that way, always taking the money back to him.

Dr. Chen, a good friend to Ezra, whispered to him one day, "Come into my room."

The Japanese had said that Ezra must not talk to his co-workers about anything except medical work. He quickly broke the rule.

"I've heard on the radio that you are going back to America," reported the Chinese doctor.

"No," replied Ezra. "I've been told that only the old people are going. I won't because I'm military age."

Dr. Chen insisted, "I've heard you are going."

Ezra soon discovered Dr. Chen had heard correctly. The United States Embassy had agreed to exchange 1,600 Japanese for 1,600 Americans.

Before long, Ezra headed homeward aboard an Italian ship, the S.S. *Conte Verde* (CONtay VERday). It sailed to Mozambique (Moe-zam-BEAK), Africa, to exchange passengers with the S.S. *Gripsholm*, another ship. Nobody on the *Conte Verde* had flags, but some found red, white, or blue ribbons. They waved them frantically as the ship steamed into the African harbor.

Officers on the British ships and those on the U.S. Merchant Marine ships recognized the *Conte Verde*. They blew their whistles loudly. Three short blasts and a long one signaled V for victory. All 1,600 Americans cried without embarrassment as the noisy welcome filled the harbor air.

Sometime later the *Gripsholm* arrived in New York without any kind of welcome for its load of returning Americans. Frances, however, stood on the dock and waited anxiously for her first glimpse of Ezra.

\* \* \*

Now that God had brought them back together, Ezra and Frances asked once again,

*Sunnyslope Farm, near Alum Creek, Ohio*

"What does God want us to do next?" Trying to find the answer occupied them as they relaxed at Sunnyslope Farm in Ohio.

Finally they decided, "We could open a new medical practice in Columbus. It's not far away."

Ezra mentioned their plans one day as he shopped in Weaver's Red and White Store in Marengo.

"In Columbus?" asked Charlie Weaver. "Why not here in Marengo? Remember, there's no doctor in this part of the county."

Later, as Ezra had his hair cut, men in the barbershop said the same. So did the clerks at the hardware store.

"You're more than welcome to live here at Sunnyslope," said Uncle Elbert. His second wife, Mary, agreed.

Ezra and Frances soon had all their arrangements completed. They moved their belongings into Sunnyslope, and at last the tiny town of Marengo, Ohio, had a new doctor.

Residents quickly passed the news that Dr. Ezra DeVol delivered babies, made house calls day or night, and treated all kinds of injuries and illnesses. He also did everything he could to help his patients know about God's love and His willingness to forgive their sin.

Ezra cared for Uncle Elbert when he became ill. Mary told the DeVols after Uncle Elbert died, "My husband wanted you and Charles and Catherine to have Sunnyslope. From now on it's yours."

Dr. Isabella's children remembered for the rest of their lives the kindness of Elbert and Martha Benedict, distant relatives known to them as uncle and aunt.

On February 24, 1944, the arrival of their new baby, Joseph Edward DeVol, delighted Ezra and Frances. Philip Edmund's birth three years later brought equal happiness to the family.

Life in the big, roomy house at Sunnyslope pleased the DeVols. They cherished the times they could eat meals together. The children loved the huge lawn and farmyard with plenty of space to roll in crunchy fall leaves or flop in the feathery-soft winter snow.

Every morning they all gathered in the living room. Ezra read from the Bible, then everyone knelt to pray. Pris, Pat, Joe, and Phil grew up learning how to tell God about their everyday activities.

Frances sometimes sang solos at the Alum Creek Friends Church where the family attended Sunday school and worship services. Now and then she helped her busy husband in his office. People also knew her as a gracious hostess, whose six-bedroom farmhouse often overflowed with guests.

"I want to be like Mother when I grow up," said Pris.

"I do, too," Pat agreed. They had already noticed how their mother always knew what to do, and that she did everything with a special touch.

"God's presence honors their home," a friend once said.

Ezra and Frances talked about the young people of their community. "Somebody needs to do something to help them," said Ezra.

"Too many of them are having babies before they're married," Frances said. She and Ezra asked God to show them what they could do.

In 1946, Ezra and Frances attended a meeting of Youth for Christ leaders in Medicine Lake, Minnesota. They talked with Billy Graham as well as others while there. Afterward, the DeVols went back home full of good ideas.

"Let's begin Saturday night meetings for young people," they suggested to nearby pastors. "We could have the meetings every other week."

Many people helped with the peppy meetings that often featured guest musicians. Years afterward, the DeVols still thought about the teenagers who had received Jesus as their Savior at those meetings. "Those were good times," they said.

Although they enjoyed their busy, satisfying life at Sunnyslope, Ezra and Frances decided in 1948 to go back to China. "The war's been over long enough now, so this is a good time to go," said Ezra.

Another doctor took over the growing medical practice. Special friends moved to Sunnyslope to care for the farm. The DeVols headed to California to board a ship. Once there, they discovered the dock workers had gone on strike. They could not leave on schedule.

Before long, missionaries from China arrived. "The Communists have entered China," they said. "We couldn't stay any longer."

Another change of plans. "What next?" Ezra and Frances asked themselves again. They and the children settled into a home for missionaries in Oakland, California, as they decided what to do.

They heard from friends in Ohio who advised, "Come back here and practice medicine again." Someone else invited Ezra and Frances to start a new mission in Japan. The Mission Board from Ohio Yearly Meeting of Friends sent a letter to ask, *Will you go to India?*

*Chhatarpur Hospital where Ezra and Frances DeVol worked for many years*

"God asked us to go to China, not India," Ezra told Frances. "On the other hand, maybe we should think about it."

"Why don't we each go somewhere and pray alone about it," Frances suggested.

After a while they got together and compared ideas. "God showed me Isaiah 30:21," said Ezra. "'This is the way; walk in it.'"

Frances laughed and it sounded like music. "Guess what? That's the same verse God showed me."

That settled the matter. "God has opened a new way for us," they said.

They unpacked their cold-weather clothes intended for China and bought hot-weather items for India. They also bought hospital equipment and a Dodge Carry-All to use as an ambulance.

A few weeks later, on April 6, 1949, the six DeVols arrived in Bombay, India. They stepped off the ship into 105 degree heat. "This is the hottest place I've ever been," said Ezra, wiping sweat off his face.

Everett and Catherine Cattell had traveled south from Chhatarpur to welcome them. "We'll load the Dodge with your baggage," Everett said, "and I'll drive to Chhatarpur."

"I'll go on the train with the rest of you," said Catherine.

Scorching winds blew dust and soot into the open windows of the railroad car. The sight of the unfamiliar countryside suddenly overwhelmed Ezra.

*Everything's so different from China*, he thought. *I don't know if I'm up to this job or not.* Since Frances and the others had gone to another compartment for lunch, Ezra knelt by himself to pray. Moments later, one of God's promises came to mind: "My Presence will go with you, and I will give you rest." Later he would open his Bible and look up that promise in Exodus 33:14.

Ezra took a deep breath and got up from his knees. All at once he looked forward to whatever would happen as they lived and worked on the plains of India.

## Chapter 7

# THE BROKEN-DOWN BIKE

"We're happier than we've ever been," Ezra said ten days after arriving in India. "After all, we're where God wants us."

The DeVols completed a quick tour to Chhatarpur, Gulganz, Bijawar, and a little village called Ghari. Then they boarded the bus to Landour. The nerve-racking 26-mile ride swung them around curves that bent back on themselves. At the end of the line, coolies loaded the DeVol's baggage onto their backs. Ezra and Frances gasped as these strong Indian men carried their heavy loads up a steep trail to Rosebank Cottage.

As Ezra and Frances slowly climbed up the path, they stopped to admire the spectacular view. They had never seen anything as grand as the jagged mountains that formed a ring around the broad valley far below.

Language study at Landour challenged them. "I can't hear the Hindustani tones distinctly," Ezra moaned. "It's impossible for me to say them right. It's a lot easier to think in Chinese."

Eventually he and Frances finished their language study and moved to Chhatarpur, located on the plains of the Bundelkhand District. Right away they visited Chhatarpur Christian Hospital. Dr. Grace Singh, the first Indian woman doctor in the region, welcomed them. Samson Huri Lal, the first male nurse on the staff, did, too.

The hospital sat on land given by a maharaja many years before. This local ruler had wanted sick women and children to have medical treatment. People in the United States gave money and prayed. Now, the 30-bed hospital gave hope to thousands of people.

Ezra became the Hospital Medical Superintendent. Frances started out as Superintendent of Nurses. They gathered with the staff each morning at seven o'clock to hear the report given by the night nurse. Next, they went with the staff into the wards for devotions. The nurses took turns choosing the hymn, giving a short thought, and leading in prayer.

Other missionaries helped Ezra and Frances learn about Indian life. "India has several classes of people, each called a *caste*," someone explained. "Indians can never change from the caste they're born into, and the caste completely controls their lives. That's why it's hard for Indians to become Christians."

The Brahmins, or priestly caste, rated at the top. Next came the rulers. Below them ranked the business people and the farmers. Outcastes, sometimes called untouchables, made up the lowest class. That caste included more than half the people in Bundelkhand.

"Even the untouchables fight to gain a higher standing among themselves," said missionary Anna Nixon.* "I once heard an outcaste woman with two chapatis in her hand screaming at another outcaste woman. 'You stupid old woman! You touched me! You've ruined my bread. Now what will I eat all day?'"

Anna continued. "Another time, I patted some children on their heads. They laughed and ran away. That night one of them told me, 'I'm an untouchable, so I didn't have to take a bath after you touched me today. The others did, though.'"

Ezra and Frances wondered, *Will we ever understand this caste system*?

Ezra first did surgery at Chhatarpur Christian Hospital on November 18, 1949. He soon performed several surgeries each day, as well as treated illnesses. Frances worked at the hospital many hours a day, too. Often she went back later to help with emergency surgeries.

She and Ezra missed Pris and Pat, who had gone away to Woodstock School at Landour. They

*Read about Anna Nixon's missionary life in* Whistling Bombs and Bumpy Trains, *also by Betty M. Hockett.*

knew that in a few years Joe and Phil would also go to school there.

"We need a men's ward," Ezra declared one day. "The Indians believe men shouldn't have medical attention in the same place as women and children. It's awkward to have to treat men out on the back porch."

Right away he and Everett Cattell decided to visit other mission hospitals. "We'll find out how their staffs treat both men and women," said Ezra.

A local district commissioner then loaned a large tent to use as a men's ward temporarily. At the same time, many people in the United States prayed for a new addition to the hospital. Some sent money, and construction started.

On Monday, March 10, 1951, the new Williams Ward for male patients opened at Chhatarpur Christian Hospital. Sick men and boys soon filled all sixteen beds.

Ezra examined one skinny man who could barely move. "You're starved for good food," Ezra said.

He could barely hear the man explain, "Monkeys got most of my food. I didn't dare kill them because they're sacred. One monkey can eat almost as much as I do."

"Oh my," said Ezra, shaking his head.

On another day, Suratiya Bai arrived at the hospital in an open wagon. She had had a rough ride all the way from her village. Ezra took one look at the tiny woman. She made him think of a rubber ball with arms, legs, and a head. "This is unbelievable," he said.

The doctors and nurses examined Suratiya Bai. They measured her waist, swollen by a huge growth. "Sixty-five inches," said Frances.

"I haven't been able to walk for two months," Suratiya said.

Ezra drained eleven gallons of fluid from the growth. A few days later he said, "Now we can operate."

The staff prayed before the operation. "I have faith in Jesus," whispered Suratiya Bai. Ezra removed the growth, which weighed 20 pounds. "Counting the fluid, she carried 108 pounds of extra weight," he said.

Suratiya Bai stayed in the hospital to get well. The Indian Bible woman visited her every day.

At last Ezra said, "You're well enough to go back to your village now."

Suratiya Bai looked pleased. "I'll tell all my relatives and friends these verses the Bible woman helped me learn," she said. "I'll keep on praying, too. The Bible woman taught me how to talk to God."

Sometimes patients heard wild stories about the hospital from friends or relatives who did not really know what went on there. Rather than telling the truth, those patients gave excuses for not staying at the hospital. "My house has just burned." "My home has been robbed, and I have just had word of it." "My son (or daughter) is about to be married." "My father has just died." "The priest says it is not a good time."

Sometimes patients died in the hospital, in spite of the good care Ezra, Frances, and the rest of the staff gave them.

Once a woman died after giving birth to her baby in the hospital. Raja Bai, a young Christian, could hardly believe her sister had died in the Chhatarpur Hospital. "You have murdered my sister!" she shouted at the Indian doctor. Other Christian members of the family felt bitter about the death, too. They yelled more false complaints.

Ezra and Frances felt sorry, also. They went to the village where Raja Bai and her husband, Nathu, lived. They sat with the young couple beside their well and listened as Nathu and Raja Bai talked. The DeVols encouraged them. They gave them advice about the education of their children.

Gradually, Nathu and Raja Bai drew closer to God. Soon, more of their relatives also became Christians.

\* \* \*

Every day Ezra saw ugly, smelly sores on legs, itchy skin, infected eyes, malaria, asthma, tuberculosis, and cases of bronchitis.

Once Ezra wrote in a letter, *Medical work gives us an opportunity to love, bless, and do good. We hope that as we show love, folks will have some idea what we mean when we talk about love.*

Ezra did not spend all of his time at the hospital. Early each Wednesday morning he rode his motorbike 22 miles from Chhatarpur to Gulganj. After tea with missionaries Cliff and Betty Robinson, he saw patients at their brick-and-stone clinic.

Ezra would then ride 33 miles to Amarmau, where other missionaries, Milton and Rebecca Coleman, worked. He saw patients until noon, then had lunch with the Colemans. Afterward, more patients lined up for Ezra's attention. When he had seen all of them, Ezra hurried back to Gulganj for late afternoon clinic followed by another cup of tea with Robinsons. On his way back to Chhatarpur later, he stopped along the road to tend to little groups of people who flagged him down.

Ezra's village patients sat on a chair as he examined them. One Indian woman took a look at the chair and refused to sit. "She probably has never sat on a chair before," Ezra whispered to the other missionaries. "And she's not about to learn now."

"My arm hurts," complained one man.

Ezra examined him, and said, "A decayed tooth is your main problem. I'll pull it for you."

When the man realized what the doctor planned to do, he jumped up and ran away, bad tooth and all.

Another man announced he had come a long way. Ezra asked in his usual manner, "What's the problem?"

"Oh, nothing," replied the man. "I just came to have a look at the doctor."

Sometimes villagers showed their appreciation to Ezra by bending down to touch his feet. "I wish they wouldn't do that," he said to the missionary helping him.

A long time later, one missionary coworker wrote, *I felt the same kind of respect for Ezra as the villagers did.*

On the way home one Wednesday, Ezra's motorbike suddenly quit. No matter how hard he tried to start it, nothing happened. He took the engine apart after several more tries. He cleaned the spark plug and the carburetor and put everything back together again. Still it would not start. The doctor took everything apart and cleaned the plug and carburetor a second time.

Nothing happened then, either.

Ezra sat down beside the road to wait for someone to come along. *Not many people travel this road*, he thought, looking to the right and to the left. *It's getting dark, and I'm 37 miles from home.*

He sat there, wondering what to do. *I'm out here on God's business. I can surely expect Him to help me. I'll dare to pray an unusual prayer.*

Ezra stood up, put on his gloves, and straddled the motorbike. "In the name of the Lord Jesus I command this machine to start," he said out loud.

He kicked the starter. The machine coughed feebly. Putt--puttity--putt-putt-putt-putt! With barely enough power, the motorbike slowly putt-putted down the road.

Ezra's mind pictured the road ahead. Up one hill, then down and onto level ground. If only he could make it over that hill. From there on he

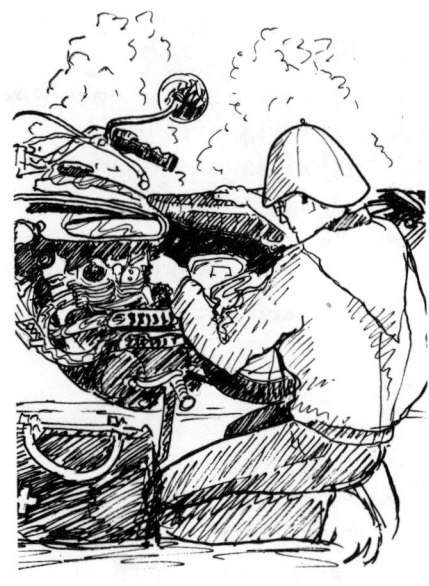
*Ezra works on the broken-down motorbike.*

wouldn't have any trouble getting home. He pulled the choke out as far as it would go. The motor coughed and sputtered uncertainly.

"This seems ridiculous," Ezra muttered. "If the Lord can make this bike work He can make it work properly." He pushed the choke back in and prayed boldly once more. "I command you in the name of the Lord Jesus Christ to work properly."

Instantly the motorbike leaped forward with a roar. Ezra almost slid off backwards. He had no more delays the rest of the way home.

Another Wednesday a few weeks later, Ezra's motorbike quit again. This time he did not bother to get out the tool kit. "I know how to get this thing started," he told himself.

As before, he commanded the bike to go in the name of the Lord Jesus. Nothing happened.

"Maybe I had better look at the engine," he said.

He opened the engine. There, in plain sight, lay a speck of carbon. Ezra cleaned off the carbon, closed the engine, and kicked the starter. The motor gave no more trouble.

\* \* \*

"Maybe we should name Chullu the-boy-who-never-smiles," Ezra said to Frances. "He acts like he doesn't expect to receive any joy from living."

"He probably doesn't," said Frances. "After all, he's only fourteen, and he's already blind."

"I'm sure he hurts all over," Ezra added. "He has those horrible sores on his face and diabetes besides. We'll have to do something about all that before we can operate on his eyes."

Day after day Chullu sat quietly, speaking only if spoken to. "I feel helpless in this case," Ezra admitted. That evening, he prayed, "Lord, help me give sight to Chullu."

He operated on Chullu's eyes later that week.

Four days after the surgery, Ezra and Samson Huri Lal, the male nurse, stood beside Chullu's bed. They prepared to remove his bandages.

Soon they would know if Chullu could see.

## Chapter 8

# TWO MAD BEARS

"Yes, oh yes. I see light," declared Chullu, closing his eyes again.

Ezra still saw no expression on the face of this fourteen-year-old. He and the nurse stood quietly waiting. Moments later the boy opened his eyes wide.

"I see your hand," he said.

"How many fingers do you count?" asked Ezra.

"Two."

"Now how many?"

"Three."

"What do you see in my hand?" Ezra asked, holding up Indian money.

"An eight anna piece," Chullu replied. At last, a smile turned his sad face into a happy one.

"What a wonderful change," said Ezra.

Chullu closed his eyes so Ezra could tape new bandages in place. The boy's face hung onto the smile. His life had started over again.

Soon, he had glasses to help him see better. Before he left the hospital, he learned to read. He also received Jesus as his Savior, making his new life complete.

Every day Ezra saw diseases he had never seen in his Ohio medical practice—smallpox, cholera, bubonic plague, and typhoid fever. Surgery took up a lot of his time, also.

Frances had more than enough to do as head nurse and assistant to both Ezra and Dr. Singh. She also taught good health care to the nurses.

At the end of one busier-than-usual day, she sank into a chair and sighed. "What pathetic cases we've seen today," she said.

"I wish everyone had soap," said Ezra.

"Soap and water would help a lot of our patients stay healthy," Frances agreed.

Ezra added, "I hope I don't ever think of my patients as problems. I often ask the Lord to help me smile at them. After all, they're people who need to see Jesus. They want love and understanding just like we do."

\* \* \*

The DeVols spent time in the United States in 1956. When they returned to India, Ezra discovered Dr. Singh had resigned from her job at the Christian Hospital.

"She has opened her own clinic in another place," someone told him.

Now, the hospital had just one doctor. He and Frances, along with the other nurses, asked God to send more help. Friends in the United States prayed, too.

Then, two Indian doctors joined their staff in the spring of 1957. Dr. Mategaonker and Dr. Shrisunder, both young men, quickly fit into the hectic schedule. Ezra wrote to people who had prayed for more help. *We thank God He has again answered prayer. We're grateful for these young men who care for sick bodies and who also pray for their patients.*

By this time, Joe and Phil had gone away to Woodstock School along with Pris and Pat. Ezra and Frances looked forward to the times their family could get together at Chhatarpur in the winter or at Landour in the summer.

They all loved to ride their bikes into the Indian countryside after church on Sunday. In good weather, they packed a picnic lunch to enjoy alongside one of the beautiful lakes. Sometimes Frances would pop corn in the evenings, and Ezra would amuse everyone with his funny stories and antics.

\* \* \*

Ezra went hunting with other missionary men as often as he could. Once in a while he brought home good meat for the family. At other times, he had a different reason for hunting.

"Milton Coleman tells me tigers are killing some of the villagers' cattle out near Amarmau," Ezra said to Clifton Robinson one day.

"That's right," Clifton agreed. "Let's go out and try to get a shot at the tiger."

Ezra and Clifton hired Indian guides and beaters, who led them to a wild and hilly spot. A big tree overlooked a dry river bed. The guides fixed a perch for Ezra in the tree while Clifton hurried off to watch and wait elsewhere.

The beaters banged sticks together, hoping the noise would drive out any wild animals hiding nearby. Half an hour later, Ezra heard the beaters shout, "Panther! Panther!"

Ezra's heart raced. Which way would the panther come? He scanned the territory, his gun in the firing position. Suddenly he saw two big black shapes running side by side.

*Oh, oh!* thought Ezra. *Sloth bears. The worst-tempered animals in the jungle. They'll charge for no reason at all. It's no wonder the villagers don't like 'em.*

The bears came closer. As they ran beneath his tree, Ezra fired. The bullet hit low. It passed through the belly skin of one bear and into the other. Both bears immediately roared, sending echoes every direction. They reared up on their hind legs and lunged at each other. The war began.

Ezra laughed as he watched the battle below. *They both think the other one has done something.*

Suddenly, he choked on his laugh. The two mad bears got closer to his tree. Would they take their fight on up into it?

## Chapter 9

# HEADING NORTH

"Hey, you guys!" Ezra yelled to the bears. "There's not enough room up here for all three of us!"

He aimed and fired. The bears dropped dead underneath the tree.

Ezra whistled with relief. "That's two bears the villagers won't have to worry about."

Later his Indian beaters told him, "The panther heard all the commotion and took off the other direction."

No one saw the tiger, either.

\* \* \*

One morning, Ezra read Deuteronomy 2:3 for his morning devotions. He thought about what he had just read. "You have made your way around this hill country long enough; now turn north."

North! That made him think of Nepal, the tiny country at the top of India. He had heard that the United Mission to Nepal needed a surgeon in its hospital in Kathmandu. Sick people traveled many days to the big city hospital only to hear, "We can't treat you because we have no qualified surgeon."

*Does this verse mean we should think about going to Nepal?* Ezra asked the Lord.

He and Frances thought and prayed about Nepal for the next few months. During that time, they received an official invitation to the hospital there.

The DeVols read their Bibles and asked God what He wanted them to do. At last they understood. "God wants us to work in Nepal," Ezra told their coworkers. "Dr. Mategaonker and Dr. Shrisunder can manage the work here at Chhatarpur while we're gone."

The Friends mission in India gave permission for Ezra and Frances to go ahead and work in Nepal for a few weeks. Joe and Phil came from Woodstock School to go with them. The four of them arrived in Kathmandu on January 19, 1959.

Ezra took a deep breath of the cold air. "This reminds me of China," he said, already feeling at home.

The magnificent peaks of the Himalaya mountains, the world's highest, towered above the Kathmandu Valley. With warm India to the south and cold, dry Tibet to the north, most of Nepal's population lived throughout the hills and lower plains. The ordinary Nepalese had no contact with the rest of the world.

For a long time, the government of Nepal had forbidden outsiders to work there. Only recently, authorities had given permission for a few people to come to Nepal and work. Missionaries from several countries had then grouped together to run the Shanta Bhawan Hospital, located in an old palace.

Their first day in Kathmandu, the DeVols moved into one room in the hospital. "Years ago the king's children used this room as a playhouse," someone explained.

"What a view!" exclaimed Frances as she looked out the window at the dazzling sight of the tall, white-topped mountains.

Before the day ended, Ezra and Frances met the doctors, nurses, technicians, radiologists, and pharmacists. They also toured the hospital.

"Our 135 beds are constantly full," one of the doctors said. "The medical needs here are five times greater than in India."

The DeVols went to work right away. Ezra operated three days a week with Frances helping. Joe painted the X-ray room, and Phil typed reports in the hospital office.

One morning Dr. Edgar Miller called Ezra into the examining room. "This man was injured four days ago when he fell from a bicycle. See what you think."

Ezra quickly felt the man's pulse. His experienced fingers picked up only a faint tremor instead of a steady beat. He took the patient's blood pressure and found it unusually low. The man, whose face had already turned blue, lay deadly quiet, making no response.

"It's too late to do anything," said Ezra. "He's about to die."

"Can't you do *something*?" Dr. Miller asked.

Ezra stared at the patient. *Lord, do You want me to do something with this man who's going to die any minute now?*

Suddenly Ezra had an idea. "I'll do a lumbar puncture to get some of the extra fluid off," he whispered. As soon as he inserted the sterile needle into the man's spine, Ezra noticed that the patient breathed more normally. His blood pressure improved, and his face slowly took on its usual golden color.

"We can operate now," Ezra said. "If we relieve the pressure on his brain, he has a chance to live."

Dr. Miller called the surgery team together. They talked about the operation, then agreed to do it. "It's risky," they told the man's family. "He might die on the operating table. If we don't do surgery, though, we know he'll die soon."

The relatives understood. "He was at the government hospital, but they don't do surgery there," one of them explained. "The doctors said he would die soon, so we decided to take him to the sacred Bagmati River. We wanted to put his feet in the water so he could go straight to heaven when he died. But when we got as far as your hospital, we decided to see if anyone here could help him."

Nurses prepared the man for surgery. The team prayed and began the delicate operation on his brain. Ezra removed a blood clot as big as a lemon.

"I don't know if he'll live or die, but I've done all I can," he said.

The next morning Ezra hurried to the man's room. Immediately the nurse blurted out, "He's remarkably better. We've seen what God can do."

The patient recovered. His friends and family who had hated Christianity and the western world changed their minds. Newspapers carried articles about the operation, the first time in Kathmandu a doctor had opened up a man's head.

"We thank the Lord for this case," said Ezra. "It's brought goodwill for the mission and for Christians."

When one of King Mahendra's assistants needed gallbladder surgery, Ezra performed the operation. He received a message in the operating room as he finished.

"It's a note from the king," Ezra reported. "He wants to see the gallbladder I've just removed."

Ezra asked a worker to deliver it. Later, the king informed Ezra, "I opened the gallbladder and discovered two-hundred and eighty-eight gallstones inside."

"Our king is interested in medicine and science," explained another Nepali. "Sometimes he and the queen go with the doctors to visit patients in the hospital."

Ezra and Frances enjoyed Bible studies with the missionaries and worship with the Nepalese staff who loved to sing. "We like it whether we understand what they say or not," said Frances.

The busy days passed quickly and soon the DeVols returned to their duties at Chhatarpur. Ezra told his friends there, "I performed 185 operations in Nepal. These have been some of the happiest weeks of our lives."

For the next few years, Ezra and Frances traveled back and forth from Kathmandu to Chhatarpur several times a year. Arranging for the necessary travel permits for each trip could have proved difficult. Nepal's Major General, the officer in charge of such affairs, solved that problem.

After Ezra operated on the Major General's wife, the officer told him, "You don't need to come to my office for help. Just come to my house."

Later, Ezra and Frances received a letter from the chairman of the United Mission to Nepal. *We would like you to come to work at our hospital in Kathmandu full-time. We believe you have the abilities we need.*

Ezra took a deep breath and said quietly, "I wish we could work full-time in both Nepal and India."

He and Frances prayed and talked and prayed and talked. They asked advice from the mission staff at Chhatarpur. Finally the DeVols felt God's guidance, and they accepted the invitation to Nepal. The American Friends Mission released them, asking them to visit Chhatarpur two times a year for the next three years.

The DeVols knew the amount of work that lay ahead. *How can we manage it all?* they asked themselves. As they arrived in Kathmandu on August 13, 1963, they remembered Psalm 34:4: "I sought the Lord, and he answered me; he delivered me from all my fears."

New laws went into effect in Nepal four days later. People who tried to disrupt the traditional Hindu religion would face a jail sentence or fines. They might even have to leave the country.

"These new laws will make it difficult for us to work," said Ezra.

"Yes," Frances answered. "After all, we're here to show others the way to Jesus."

"If the officials enforce the laws we may have to leave," remarked one of the other missionaries.

Ezra, the new Director of the United Mission Medical Center in Shanta Bhawan Hospital, added, "But we'll respect the law." He and the staff asked God to show them how they could continue to tell others about God's love.

Sometimes Ezra and Frances watched as Buddha worshipers tried to contact God by waving a prayer flag or spinning a prayer wheel. A ten-day ceremony included the sacrifice of 25 buffaloes and 50 goats.

At Christmastime, Ezra suggested, "Let's hold a ten-day celebration here in our hospital compound."

The workers agreed, and soon the hospital halls filled with the music of Christmas. Someone hung colorful Christmas posters in each room. Church people acted out the manger scene, complete with live sheep, lambs, and doves. The pastor read the Bible story of Jesus' birth. Outsiders showed up to watch and listen.

On Christmas Eve, the staff marched through the wards. Each person carried a lighted candle as the group sang. One member of the royal family walked beside Ezra, sharing a hymnbook with him. A Christmas message and prayer in every ward completed the evening. "Not one Nepali objected to our celebration," Ezra mentioned later.

Workers from the Russian Embassy in Kathmandu often came to the Shanta Bhawan hospital for treatment. Those admitted to the hospital found on their bedside table a Bible in their own language. "You may take the Bible home with you," Ezra always told them.

\* \* \*

At eleven o'clock one evening, Ezra received a phone call. He explained to Frances afterward, "I've been asked to go to the palace to see the king's mother. She's suffering with severe back pains."

Two workers went with Ezra to the palace. The guard at the gate said, "I must have the king's permission before I can let you in."

Ezra and the others waited at the guardhouse for the next thirty minutes. Finally, the guard unlocked the gates and allowed the guests to go into the grounds. At the palace door, another guard said, "You must take off your shoes before you enter."

Inside, the third guard escorted them into the Queen Mother's elaborately decorated room. Ezra greeted her, then did a thorough examination. *I don't want to make the wrong diagnosis*, he thought.

Finally he discovered the problem and gave his patient the necessary shot. "I'll come again," he promised.

On the next visit, Ezra and his medical workers did not have to wait so long at the gate. No one asked them to remove their shoes until they got to the top of the stairs.

They had to stop at the gate just long enough to identify themselves on the fourth visit. They did not have to take their shoes off until they reached the Queen Mother's bedroom. As they visited with his mother, King Mahendra stepped into the room and entered into the conversation.

On the final visit, no one asked Ezra and the others to remove their shoes anywhere. "We're grateful for your help," said the Queen Mother. King Mahendra, agreed, then offered coffee to the visitors.

\* \* \*

"The helicopter's waiting," said Ezra. "It shouldn't take too long for us to fly up to Tansen and evacuate a sick missionary."

He hurried out to board the large aircraft. The blades began to whirr.

"What do you know about this hospital up at Tansen?" asked the pilot. "I've never been there."

"I haven't either, but I've heard it has a peculiar roof," Ezra replied. "It's inverted to catch the rain water." The helicopter lifted straight up, then headed to the small mountain settlement.

Sometime later the pilot peered down at the landscape and said, "The hospital ought to be here somewhere."

Ezra stared down, also. He did not see anything that looked like Tansen. "I know we've come the right direction," he assured the pilot. "We'll surely see that strange roof any moment now."

They flew low over hills and valleys, turning to get a good look at the bare, rough territory from all angles. Ezra checked his watch. "We're long overdue," he said.

The insides of his hands began to sweat. His heart thumped a drum beat in his chest. Did they have enough fuel to stay in the air until they found Tansen? Or had they missed the place entirely?

## Chapter 10

# WE'VE COME A LONG WAY

"There it is!" Ezra exclaimed in a shaky voice. "There's the inverted roof." Nothing had ever looked so good as the sight of that long, white hospital with smaller buildings standing like stair steps alongside.

The pilot landed the helicopter on a level spot of ground. People crowded close to watch as hospital workers quickly carried out two patients— the sick missionary and a Nepali woman who needed surgery.

They made the trip back to Kathmandu without any problems.

\* \* \*

Frances worked alongside Ezra in the operating room every Thursday. She also helped him on days the other surgeons could not. "Frances is my first and best assistant," said Ezra. "She always knows which instrument I need and exactly when to give it to me."

Sometimes during an operation, Ezra asked Frances, "Have we ever seen a case like this before?"

If they had, she would tell him who, when, and where, as well as what they had done for the patient. "Her memory's better than mine," Ezra always said.

A Russian man once visited Ezra's office. The visitor saw a Russian Bible on the corner of the desk. "You have a Russian book here," he said.

"Yes," replied Ezra.

"May I have it?"

"Yes." Afterward, Ezra privately thanked God the Russian visitor had seen the Bible. "That's exactly what I had hoped would happen," he said.

As Director of the Medical Center, Ezra had to attend many government social events. Once he and Frances accepted an invitation to a special celebration on the grounds of the Indian Embassy in Kathmandu. Shortly after they arrived, Ezra noticed a man zigzagging through the crowd toward him. The man kept glancing over his shoulder.

"I remember him," Ezra whispered. "He was one of the Russian patients in our hospital. I can tell by the way he's acting he doesn't want anyone to see him talking to us."

The man edged closer to Ezra, with another look behind him. "Several of us at our Russian Embassy are reading your book," he whispered quickly.

"My book?" Ezra asked. Then he remembered. "Oh, yes. You mean the Bible."

* * *

The DeVols hosted a weekly Wednesday evening prayer meeting in their home. Many of the hospital staff came to pray for Nepalese leaders. Ezra and Frances also continued their daily habit of praying by themselves.

They regularly visited Prem Pradhan, a new Christian serving time in prison for converting from Hinduism. Ezra and Frances often gave him a copy of the *Good News* magazine that Prem shared with his cell mates. They took food to him, also, including a full dinner on Christmas.

The prison guard stopped them and demanded, "You must taste everything first. I will make sure you have not poisoned the food."

The guard watched closely while Ezra and Frances ate bites of everything they had brought. Satisfied that the food would not harm his prisoner, the guard said, "It's all right. Give him the food."

* * *

In March of 1966, a serious eye problem ended the DeVol's quick-paced routine in Nepal.

"I can hardly see!" Ezra declared one day. "I'm afraid my right eye has a detached retina."

The hospital staff immediately prayed, then helped make arrangements for Ezra and Frances to fly to the United States. Once they reached

Cleveland, Ohio, Ezra had surgery on his right eye. Later, the doctors removed a cataract from his left eye. His right eye, however, did not heal completely.

"Can we ever work as a surgical team again?" Ezra and Frances wondered. The situation looked gloomy to both of them as the months went by.

One day Ezra read his Bible and then said, "God has spoken to me. However my eyesight turns out, I want to live with peace in my soul."

"You've encouraged me a lot," Frances said. Her laugh sounded like music again.

Soon, Ezra's right eye began to improve. Several months later his doctor said, "Your eyes are doing well now. You may return to India."

Before they left, Ezra and Frances spent time with each of their children. Priscilla, a nurse married to Tom Cox, brought her Stephanie, Geoffery, and Bill to see them. Patricia, a teacher married to Russell Haynes, made sure her parents got acquainted with little Michael. Phil had enrolled in Malone College at Canton, Ohio.

Later that year, 1968, Ezra and Frances traveled to California to visit Joe, his wife, Judy, and their new baby, Nancy.

"We hope we can settle down for a good long stretch of service," Ezra said as they headed to India.

Back at Chhatarpur, everything about the Christian Hospital pleased Ezra and Frances. They walked through the new offices. They toured the additional wards for patients, the improved home for nurses, and the better outpatient department. "Look, Frances, proper hospital beds instead of cots, and all this new equipment, besides."

"It's all so different from the first time we saw it," she said. "Remember the times Joe had to hold the flashlight while you operated on a patient?"

Ezra nodded and chuckled, "And you had to pump the little kerosene stove to pressure cook the syringes to make them sterile? We've come a long way."

Sometime later, city officials asked Ezra to give a speech for a United Nations celebration. He prepared thoroughly and set out for the occasion with notes in hand. As the program concluded, Ezra wondered why the people in charge had not called on him to speak.

"Why did I go to all that work to get my speech ready?" he mumbled to himself.

\* \* \*

"One, two... fifteen... twenty-one... thirty-three..." Stacks of syringes and medicine bottles grew higher as Frances counted items in central supply on the morning of January 17, 1972.

All at once Frances grabbed her chest. "I can't take any more," she whispered.

Ezra rushed to her side. He examined her quickly, then did more tests. "You've had a heart attack, Frances," said Ezra. "I'm going to take you to Delhi to see doctors there."

The day they left, Pastor Stuti Prakash came to pray with them. Frances felt as if God stood beside her during the prayer.

The pastor said afterward, "Mrs. DeVol, God has healed you. Now you just have to gain your strength."

Dr. Roy, the heart doctor in Delhi did some of the same tests Ezra had done earlier. "I can't believe it," he said. "This EKG shows nothing wrong with your heart."

When they returned to Chhatarpur, Frances worked hard at not working hard. She did only simple nursing duties, though she wanted to do much more. She and Ezra often asked each other, "Is India too much for us? Can we keep going?"

One by one, missionaries arrived to help with the work. They encouraged Ezra and Frances to go to the United States for that summer.

"We'll come back to India in August," Ezra said.

A few weeks later in Ohio, Frances fell and broke her right wrist. Ezra had a hemorrhage in his left eye, and doctors ordered him to bed. November arrived before they got back to Chhatarpur.

There the news spread quickly: "The doctor and his wife have come to pack, then leave for good."

For a long time, Ezra and Frances had hoped the hospital could add a new building. "We need a library, a reading room, and a worship center," they said. "We also could use space for classes, committee meetings, and fellowship." They prayed and gave money.

Dr. Mategaonker and Ezra dug the first shovelfuls of dirt on February 12, 1974. The building then took shape as the DeVols completed their plans to return to the United States. The hospital staff, students, church members, women, youth, missionaries, and even the servants all sponsored many special farewells.

Chhatarpur city officials invited more than 300 people to a special tea honoring Ezra and Frances. They seated the DeVols in chairs on the platform and presented them with garlands of flowers. Several people stood to read documents of appreciation. They also gave plaques engraved in both Hindi and English.

"Do you have something you wish to say?" the official in charge asked Ezra.

*This is my chance for a Christian message*, he thought. Immediately Ezra thought about the speech he had prepared but had not given at the United Nations celebration. *Now I know why I worked so hard on it before.* He stood and spoke the message stored in his mind.

"Thank you for your love and kindness. We shall always have happy memories of our work here, and we'll never forget the friends we have made over these twenty-five years. We came to India because God called us."

He spoke of how God considered all people worthwhile. "He created all people equal in their dignity and rights to be loved and honored. No one should have to be insulted. Jesus said to love Him completely, then to love our neighbors as ourselves. He will help us do this if we ask Him."

At home that night Ezra told Frances, "I don't know how many people actually heard what I said today. That was, however, the most meaningful message I ever had a chance to give to officials in Chhatarpur. For me, that's the highpoint of our years here."

Ezra and Frances stood beside the new building for one last photograph before they left. Someone lifted the cloth hanging over a bronze plaque attached to the building. The DeVols both gasped with surprise when they saw the words on the plaque.

*DeVol Fellowship Hall*

"We had no idea," they said.

The next day, Lalla Mali, their gardener, brought his family to see the DeVols. These Hindu outcastes covered Ezra and Frances with flowers. "Dr. Sahib, you have shown us the way to the Lord. Now I want to pray in Jesus' name."

He bowed his head, prayed to receive Jesus as his Savior, and gave his life and his family to God.

\* \* \*

When they returned to Ohio, the DeVols moved into the big white house at Sunnyslope, for it still belonged to Dr. Isabella's children. Ezra went to work as an assistant to another doctor in Marengo. He enjoyed learning new developments in medicine, too. Frances supported him with her prayers and encouraging words.

Life continued in this way until 1977 when they decided the time had come to retire from doctoring full-time in Ohio. God showed them what to do, and they moved to Newberg, Oregon. There, Ezra joined the staff at Newberg Community Hospital on a part-time basis. He also set up an office in Friendsview Manor, near their apartment.

Ezra and Frances prayed regularly for each member of their family. The Coxes and the Hayneses still lived in Ohio. Phil, his wife, Donna, and their children Christopher and Sarah Christine, did too. Joe and Judy lived in California. The arrival of other grandchildren had delighted Ezra and Frances: Debbie DeVol, Julia Haynes and her older sisters, Sarah and Cynthia, and Philip Cox.

The same physical problems that had brought Ezra and Frances back from India stayed on to bother. Finally, Ezra made a painful decision, "I will not renew my medical license."

The summer of 1990 began with Frances successfully recovered from a broken hip and from another heart attack. Ezra's energy gave new strength to his wife every day.

One morning everything changed. Ezra felt something unusual happening to him. At the hospital later, the doctors said, "Yes, Ezra, you have had a stroke."

From that day on, Ezra and Frances did things differently.

His legs no longer moved like they could before. He had to work hard to learn how to walk again. After a long while, Ezra could take a few steps. A cane helped hold him steady.

They moved from their apartment into Friendsview Manor. Then, the days and months went by and Ezra got stronger. He could go for longer walks with Frances strolling alongside. She willingly shared her meager strength with him. Together they gathered courage and cheerfulness. They inspired their friends.

Although much had changed for Ezra and Frances, their life interests and around-the-world prayers had not. They often thought about all that had gone before.

"God has been wonderfully good to us," Ezra said. "He always made His directions clear, and they've been such a comfort."

And so it would continue—God clearly showing the way, Ezra and Frances gladly obeying His call.

*Soon after the completion of this manuscript, Ezra had another stroke. He died on April 24, 1992.*